Teacher
Alligator

Teacher Alligator

FAUSTIN CHARLES

Illustrated by
David Wojtowycz

**BLOOMSBURY
CHILDREN'S
BOOKS**

*For Dalia, Chewan, Kysha
and Emma Matthewson*

First published in Great Britain in 2000
Bloomsbury Publishing Plc, 38 Soho Square, London, W1V 5DF

ISBN 0 7475 4760 2

Printed in England by Clays Ltd, St Ives plc

10 9 8 7 6 5 4 3 2 1

Contents

Animal School Days

School days! school ways!
We're happy to be in class
The grasshopper leaves the grass
Happy to be in school.
Although the mosquitoes moan
The monkeys groan
They're all happy to learn,
Happy to be at school.
The days are bright
Stinging ants bite
Yet they're happy to be at school.
School days! school ways!
Dogs snarl and bark
The hammerhead shark
Is happy to be in school
School days! school ways!
Even with the gorilla's unfriendly look
When he reads a book
He's still happy to be at school.
The chickens feed
But they love to read
Write and sing
Almost anything
When they're in the school-building.
School days! school ways!

We're happy to be at school.
A group of opossums
Are busy doing sums
They're happy to be at school.
School days! school ways!
Listen to the miaowing cats
Bright at their maths
They're happy to be at school.
We're all happy
Doing geography
We're happy to be at school.
School days! school ways!
We're having a lot of fun
School days! school ways!
Our learning has just begun.

Staffroom

In the staffroom
Spoons and teacups clatter
Teachers' talk and laughter
Break-times bloom
In the teachers' rest and play.
The teapot is bubbling
Biscuits crunch their way
Until the bell is ringing.
A pupil's knock
Interrupts the relaxing voices
And the leisured choices
Beat the ticking of the clock.

A coffee-break
Takes a bunch
Of cakes through to lunch.
The spooning of milk
And no sugar
Give time to remember
Classes aren't as smooth as silk.

Wet Play

Outside the playground swims in rain
Today again
Like yesterday.
The animals have to stay
Indoors
Wondering about all-fours
In the quiet and gentle games;
Their names
Colour the gloomy day;
They groom feathers and lick paws.
The horse cannot run in the hall
She'll fall

Over hyena's catch-me shout
Turning about
In the hurried call
Of the wet play.
Some scream and fret
But there's nothing to get
From the wet play.
They read and sing
Softly through fur and wing
But everything
Is still in the wet day.

Spinning Homework

The spider with clumsy writing
Gets all the homework wrong
Pages tear with each spinning
And the words are very long.
He's bright at counting flies
Building webs up to the skies
Close to the sunrise.
With feet of eight
He's never late,
But the words are always jumbled
Homework book crumpled.
Sometimes numbers spin and shake
Pencils bend and break!
Sometimes he makes a sign
With books hanging on a line.

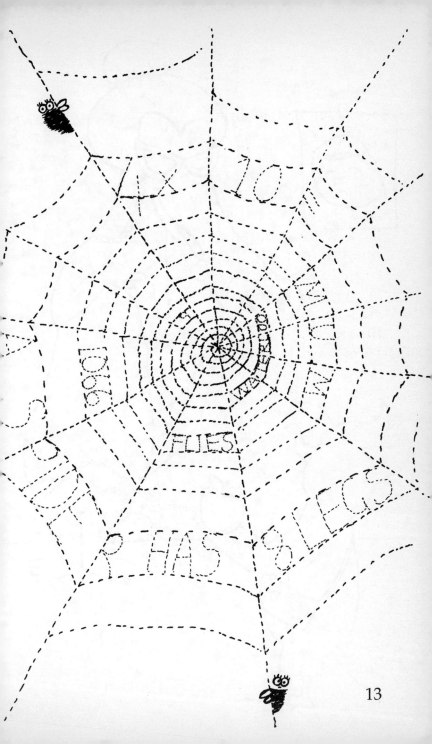

13

Parrot Pet

I parrot the teacher's words
It's only for bright birds!
Everyday I bring an apple for her
Sometimes I miss her.
She takes me under her wing
I chant and sing
The sweetest feathery verbs.
I fly around the classroom, swerve
Around her chair.
Every word and number
I learn by heart
To please her.
When lessons fall from her mouth
I repeat them inside out.
She treats words like seeds
Flowering the brain while it feeds.
When I hear the bell
I can't wait to tell
How sometimes my lessons are mirth.
She's patient as can be
Reminding me of what hard work is worth.

Pupil Snail is Slow But Bright

Pupil snail is always late
In reaching the school-gate.
The teachers rant and worry.
He always says he's sorry
That he wasn't made to hurry
And gets into an awful state.

Pupil snail is always so slow
Why does he bother to go
He says he loves school
Does not want to be a fool.
Although he takes a long time from A to C
His brain is busier than a bee.

Bookworm

I don't feed
I read.
Worming my way
Through the school library
From infancy.
Picking the leaves
From Alice to Humpty Dumpty,
I chew on each magical story
Watch Gretel tugging the Witch's sleeves.
Munching into a story bunch
I lick through the Chocolate Factory
These are the lessons for my lunch,
Crunch, books, crunch!
I roam
Books seeking out tasty pages
Word is the Worm
Climbing through all stages.

Giraffe at School

The giraffe's tall! tall! tall!
The giraffe's peeping over the school-wall.
Everything looks small
When the giraffe peeps down over the wall.
The animals like to play
Long neck reach and run away!
The giraffe tiptoes on a hoof
And puts his tongue on the roof.
The Head Teacher warns he's a fool
The giraffe licking about the school;
Poking its head in a classroom
It makes the teachers fume
Because it's all against the rules.
Tempers spray against the spotted skin
As the animals reach out then settle in.

Mary's Lamb

Mary's lamb was good at geography
Mary's lamb was great at maths
Mary's lamb came to school early
Wearing funny hats.

Mary's lamb was good at reading
Mary's lamb was great at art
Mary's lamb loved music playing
Dancing like an acrobat.

Mary's lamb was great at running
Came in first in every race
Gave football a very good kicking
Scoring goals with perfect grace.

The school made a joyous uproar!
The animals didn't laugh any more
They chanted a rhyming song:
'School is where lambs belong.'

Count His Name

The centipede merrily goes
To school and everyone knows
He's best at Arithmetic
From one to a hundred, quick!
He curls and counts his toes.
He reaches a century
And doesn't have to hurry
It's easier than wearing clothes.
Adding two noughts to a one
Does it for fun
Stinging the number as it grows.

Elephant Memory

The elephant is good at remembering
Names, books and things
And when the school-bell rings.
She never forgets a face
Always remembers her place
When the important exam begins.
She remembers last year's menu
And who ate all the carrot stew.
Who was the first Head Teacher
And the prettiest teacher.
She's a trunk of information
A trumpeting encyclopaedia.
Her memory is more than photographic
With exams she's never in a panic
She just rubs her head
And the knowledge starts to spread.

Hummingbird, the Music Teacher

Hum! hum! hum! hum!
She hums a song.
The school's song-bird sounds
A flower-gong.
Hum! hum! hum! hum!
A violin speaks on her cue
She tingles piano red, hot and blue.
Little symphony winging along
Smoothing heavenly harps down.
She sweetens at noon
Stirring each voice with her favourite tune
Hum! hum! hum! hum!
She plays the heart-strings:
An animal dances and sings.

Mosquito Inspector

Schools inspector
Insect inspector
Mosquito, the watcher
Making wrongs right
Teachers hate the stinging bite
Sometimes he visits schools at night.
His name is Hector
A great dissector
Insect inspector.
His buzz and sting
Makes the animals cringe and cling.
Lessons are always sparkling bright
Whenever he comes in sight.
It's no use spraying insecticide
Or to ring the bell and run and hide.
Shaking his head from side to side
He knows when they've worked or lied.
Work tries to be graded high
Keeping him merrily going by.

Bee Line

The bee can draw a B
Better than everybody.
She's not so good at A
It takes all day.
When it comes to a C
That may not be so easy
B is all she can see.
Her lines are so cool
The best in the school;
Her wings span the book
She doesn't have to look
As she twirls around on a stool.
Smacking nectar for lunch
Making B's in a bunch
And feasting in a honey-pool.

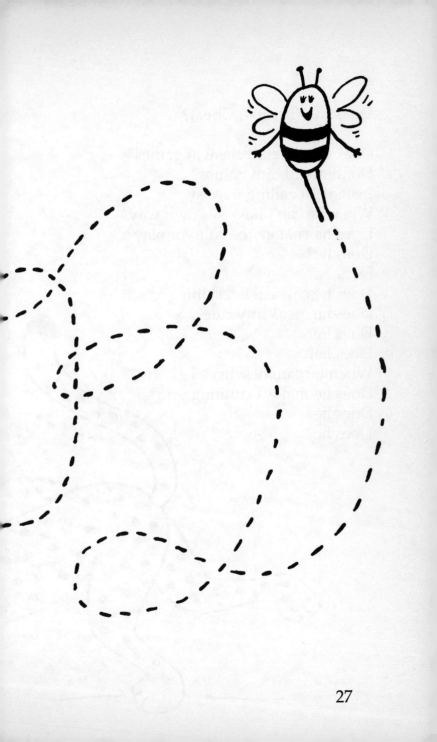

Does the Cheetah Cheat?

Does the cheetah cheat at games?
Do they call him names?
Instead of calling it a day,
When he can't have his own way,
Does he change the rules of play?
Does he?
Does he?
Does he cheat at everything at school?
Does he break any rule?
Does he?
Does he?
When he cannot win
Does he make a cunning grin?
Does he?
Does he?

Does he copy from books
And give funny looks?
When he's wrong,
Does he say he's right?
Does he snarl to fight?
Does he?
Does he?
Does he jump up and down
Wearing a frown?
Does he?
Does he?
In a playground run
Does he cheat just for fun?
Does he?
Well, does he?
Of course, he doesn't, he's tame
He's only called Cheetah by name.

French Poodle

Miss Poodle is great at teaching French
Miss Poodle is sitting on the bench.
The animals like to hear her start
She knows all the work by heart
Knows how to pronounce each noun
The animals love the way they sound
Rolling correctly off the tongue.

Her words ring out so sweetly
Catching the meaning exactly
Her pure French accent
Is like Heaven sent.

Lion in the School Library

The lion's in the library
Reading everybody.
He likes Roald Dahl
Calls him a pal.
He roars at every word
And what has happened to the dodo bird.
He examines each shelf
Pleases himself
Turning every page with a sniff.
He reads novels
About witches living in hovels
Pleased if he only gets a whiff
Of horrible history titles.
The lion never lies
When he's lying in the library
And never gets a hungry look
When his head's in a book.

Mr Dragon, the Head Master

Mr Dragon, the Head Master
Gets redder and redder.
When he's angry
He spurts fire at everybody.
The school twists and turns
Teachers scatter
For in his hot temper
Everything burns.
He flies through the air
Spitting hot air everywhere
And laughs at cries and groans.
When the fire alarm goes
He leaps and throws
The school a warning:
Lessons must all be top-scoring.

The animals made a playground rhyme
Which they sing all the time:
'Who's afraid of the Dragon Head
Fiery teeth tasting red.
Away from school it's often said
He'll get you in your bed!'

Bulldog Bully

When you first meet Bulldog bully
You have to speak nicely
He then grinds his teeth
And cuts every word with his feet.
He snaps at each sound
Growls at everyone turning round
Showing who's boss in the playground.
He barks when it's cold
Barks when it's hot
Reaching at every creature in the world.
But when a teacher is near
He whispers a fear
That bullies burst with every tear.

Our School has a Steel Band

Our school has a steel band
Every pupil lends a hand
In making it the best in the land.
Squirrel loves to play
He can do so all day.
And long-armed orangutan
Gives it a clang! bang! bang!
Chimpanzee strikes a beat
And everyone taps their feet
With the rhythms so sweet
Pan! pan! panzee!
We chant pan melody.
Zebra's notes skip and prance
Inviting us all to dance.
Fingers of sticks pounding
Out tunes spicy;

Lizard pulls chords rhyming
Tones from words nicely.
Drum beating calypso
Buffalo drumming
Armadillo booming
Keeping time with rhino.
Our school's steel band
Is very grand;
Ostrich takes its head from sand
And waves it like a magic wand,
Singing a clang! Bang! Bang!

Teacher Alligator's Roll-call

Miss Alligator
Does her register.
Begins with the widest smile
As she calls the crocodile.
Seems to swivel in her chair
Naming the grizzly bear.
Her mouth curves into a grin
Saying the name penguin.
She flicks her pen
When she calls Janey hen.
She shouts, 'Can you hear me?'
At little Jason flea.
There's always a rumpus
When she calls platypus.
She's firm
Calling to the worm.
'Present, Miss!'
A snake says with a hiss.

'I'm here!'
Answers the reindeer.
Miss Alligator is slow
To call hippo
She imagines a water game
Whenever she calls the name.
Her face shines with delight
When she comes to the kite
Knowing everything is all right.
She knows every bee
That sucks every tree
And every bird in flight.
She closes her book
With a satisfied look
For her whole class to see.

Truant Andy

Andrew ant
Is a regular truant.
The teachers rave and rant
But he just can't
Make it to school.
Says he'll never be a fool
For breaking the rule.
He spends the day
Running away
Into endless stinging play.
He has scant
Regard for the school way:
He's a true ant.
Roaming the streets
If by chance he meets
His teacher, Mr Ray
With fear
He turns from brown to grey.

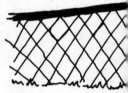

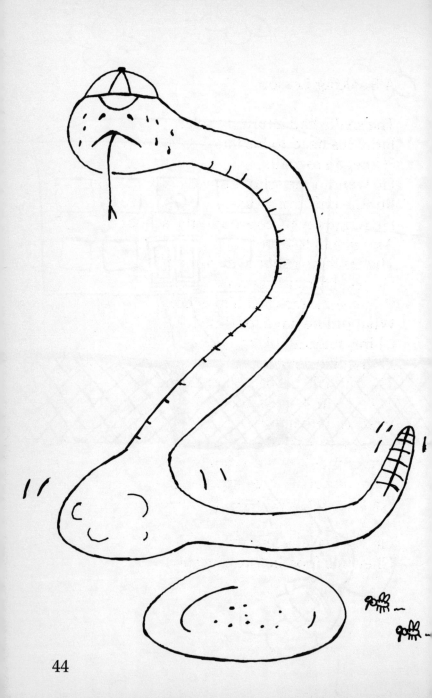

A Snaking Lesson

The snake had a tummy ache
From his head to his tail
He began to wail.
He went to the school-nurse
But the pain got worse.
He wriggled an 'S' around the school
And began to drool.
The teachers rubbed his tummy
He cried for his mummy
While standing on a high stool.
What did he have for dinner?
Chips, rice and pizza
Eating like a racer.
The animals heard him grumble
Then he took a tumble
And fell into a muddle.
Poor Sammy snake
The dinner lady told him off
Then he began to cough
And his tummy shook like a quake.

He has learnt a lesson:
Chew his food before digestion.

Our School Bus

The school bus streams along the lane
Bringing us to school again.
We laugh, talk
And sightsee
Pitying those who have to walk.
The school bus is painted yellow-and-green
The driver keeps it sparklingly clean.
Comfortably soft, cushiony seats
Our school bus beats
A sitting room scene.
Stork driver is always smiling
Through all traffic, a smooth ride
In every outing.
With his feathery map by his side
He carries us to places far and wide.
We know the bus by its sound
Outward or homeward bound;
Driving safely, watching the road,
Animals obey the highway code.

Playground Duty

Mrs Alsatian is on playground duty
Hot on the scent of everybody.
Her smile can easily
Turn into a scowl;
Whenever she has her way
Her temper can sway
Into a growl.
The animals know her grunt
When she's on the hunt
For those who are naughty;
She checks all and sundry.
She can see through walls
And when she calls
Names are answered quickly.
She ends quarrels and fights
And stops animals from falling over
They play in her sights;
Always thinking of their safety
She glances over each shoulder.

Chameleon in School

Came to school the first day
Was too shy even to play;
Somebody bawled
They couldn't see him against the wall.
He moved about cautiously
As animals circled merrily.
Some pestered him
To get away he went in a tree
And vanished on a limb.
The teacher's plea was
To be a colour she can see:
He tried his best
But the shades slipped out
When animals were being a pest.
But he was well-behaved and tidy
In class shining brightly;
The school began to love his ways
Treasuring light
By his school days.

School Outing

We went to the zoo
We enjoyed it – even moany gnu.
We saw people doing funny things
Like eating grass and frying onion-rings.
They wore rings in their noses
Rings through their lips
Chains round their hips
They couldn't smell roses.
People wore fur
To keep warm
And couldn't purr
To warn off a snow storm.
The saddest thing, of course,
We saw a man riding a horse;
Poor old Jenny mare
Just stood and stared
For a very long while
It wasn't her style
And we all feared
And shed a tear.
We saw birds in cages
Animals working for no wages
And found out about bacon and sausages.
We saw a monkey performing like a fool
A dolphin flipped stupidly in a pool

They had never been to school.
A large aquarium
Made us squirm
It was beyond belief
Gave alligator nothing but grief.

The human zoo
Was never meant for you;
In such a situation
We'll be hunted to extinction.

A Teacher's Greatest Wish

Pencils, pen, books and paper
Round black or white board so grand.
The day of the week neatly by the teacher
In a sculptured hand.
Eager faces and minds glisten
In every lesson;
Animals pay attention and listen
Food for thought, a tasty dish:
This is the teacher's greatest wish.

Animals well-behaved and orderly
Bright and yearning to have a go.
Fresh as a daisy
Answering questions and never saying no.
Respecting teachers and learning the ropes
Exercises in hard work and building-up hopes.

Learning to Count to Ten

Nought and one are one
The animals' counting game has begun.
One and one are two
So groans the gnu.
Two and one are three
Gobbles the turkey.
Three and one are four
Crows the jackdaw.
Four and one are five
Buzzes from the beehive.
Five and one are six
Barks the dog scratching ticks.
Six and one are seven
Calls the Komodo dragon.
Seven and one are eight
Splashes the slippery skate.
Eight and one are nine
Grunts the swine.
Nine and one are ten
Cackles the red hen.

57

School Bookweek

For our school's bookweek
We dressed, animal sleek,
Like characters from favourite books
Some of us had the natural looks.
Rabbit was everywhere
Sometimes she played a hare.
Birds streaked miles
Around the school
Beaks re-fashioning styles.
Fleet-footed gazelle
Was dressed like Rapunzel.
Mouse and elephant
Climbed the beanstalk
As Jack and the Giant.
The orangutan
Swung, flew and ran
Outdoing Peter Pan.
The leopard
Found it hard
To play by the book
As Captain Hook.
Woody woodpecker
Whistled a recorder
In Hamelin as the Pied-Piper.
The mouse played himself

In town and country house
From a book high on a shelf.
The hawk needed lots of room
When she squawked
Like a witch riding a broom.
A white rabbit
Ate carrots as whey
And felt comfortable as Miss Muffet:
A hamster played the spider
Keeping close to her
For a whole day.
For the elves and the shoemaker
That was left to the jaguar
He practised in class
And with grasshoppers
As elves in tall grass.
Badger played Cinderella
With fox as an ugly sister;
A rat was the prince
Who hasn't been heard from since.

Schooled into a Butterfly

Little caterpillar Caroline
Began school crying in the nursery.
She was cuddled and told that it was fine
And not to be a cry-baby.
The first day
She didn't want to play
Was afraid of noise
Didn't even play with the toys.
Slowly she changed her ways;
The teachers counted the days
As she blossomed in every class
And all the tests she had to pass.
She was the spark
That lit up the dark;
A swirling rainbow
For all to know.
The school was proud
Hers was the clever face in the crowd.
She pupated with a kiss
And became a chrysalis,
Rising Secondary high
Into the brightest butterfly.

Supply Teacher

We wonder why
The fly
Is a Supply:
With his magical ways of teaching
He could have done anything.
We never misbehave
In and out of his lessons
We're not that brave.
He waves a ruler
And sums seem easier;
His eyes pop and roll
Everything is under his control.
The class tremble but learn
Each in their turn.
Fly supply can
Teach any lesson to anyone
Under his wing
The pupils sing
Themselves to the highest things.

End of Term

The dinner ladies laughed and sang
The bell danced and rang!
Teachers were drained
Their voices strained
Calling all for a photograph.
Some uniforms were torn
Showed marks of term well-worn.
All homework was handed in
Books and neat writing
Geared to the perfect paragraph.
Parents' faces shone with delight
Pleased with every pupil in sight.
Head Teachers beamed!
Some animals streamed
A happy bark, none of their bite.
Cake, ice-cream, sweets and laughter!
The term ends not with a hungry growl
But a merry twitter.